ANNIE GISVOLD

DEDICATED ROCK-SOLID

SONGS AND POEMS

First published in 1992
by Noatun Forlag,
Trollveien 41,
N-1450 Nesodden,
Norway

Printed in Norway by Rødsten Trykkeri
Noatun Forlag
ISBN 82-992668-1-7

CONTENTS

MAYBE I'LL FIND OUT

You moved in on me so fast
that it really did impress me.
I thought: Here is a man who knows his mind!
you knew every trick o' the trade
of how to wine and dine me,
and of making me believe you're 'oh' so kind.

      What kind of rat are you?
      What kind of dog am I?
      Maybe I'll find out the day I die.

Then you turned the tables on me
just as quick as you could con me
into giving up my soul for you to keep.
Ever since you've just despised me,
ridiculed and scandalized me,
so that everyone I know thinks I'm a creep.

      What kind of clown are you?
      What kind of fool am I?
      The insult of it makes me want to cry.

Well, you're up so high above me
on a rosy powder cloud
and you're peddlin' lies about me to the angels,
while I'm down here in the cellar
where it's blacker than in hell, and where
I'm selling your Achilles to the devil.

      What kind of snake are you?
      What kind of sphinx am I?
      I hope to find it out before I die.

I NEED A MAN, YEAH!

I don't need a man to change my blown-out fuses.
I don't need a man to fix my kitchen sink,
and I don't need a man to conjure up excuses –
I don't need a man to teach me what to think.

      Don't need a man to turn me inside out!

I need a man who questions what his life is all about.

Man, don't try to take me to where all your worldly treasures lie!
I don't need a man to glue gold to my heart.
I don't need a man to kick me when his pleasures die,
and I don't need a man to set my soul apart.

      Oh man, don't park your garbage on my porch!

All I need's a man to help me light an inner torch.

I don't need a man who only sees me naked.
I don't need a man who meets my smiles with horny eyes.
Don't need a man who doesne't see that sex is all but sacred.
I don't need a man to serve me pornographic sighs.

      Oh man, don't try to nail me to the floor!

I need a man to light a spark when darkness busts my door.

I don't need a man to offend me and defend me,
and I don't need a man with a politician's bent.
I don't need a man who's always ready there to mend me
with reasons sounding like a mad practitioner's consent.

      Man, don't stick your judgment to my name!

All I need's a man who heeds and feeds the inner flame.

A SONG OF LONGING (FOR YOU)

Romanza
molto sostenuto

A bird is flying quietly,
one bird is flying high,
one is flying swiftly,
and one flies, right here, by.
      Ten are on the water
        and five are in the air.
Honey, I can't see you anywhere.

I know a bird that warbles,
and one that always sings.
I know a bird that screeches
each time she's on the wing.
      Twenty make a choir
        and three sing at my door.
Honey, I can't hear you anymore.

One bird has bright red feathers
and one is blue and white,
one's gray like stormy weather,
and one is black as night.
      Seven make a rainbow,
        and thirteen paint the clouds.
Honey, did you vanish in the crowd?

One bird sits on my shoulder
and one's perched on my head.
One bird lies on my mattress –
it acts as if it's dead.
      Thirty birds inside of me –
        through my head they soar.
Honey, I am falling through the floor.

I'M FREE !

scherzando

Strike up the music,
play up the band,
dance the conductor,
wave your magic wand!

You can touch my fingertips and you can squeeze my hair,
       I feel free like a bird in the air!

Got to pay my bills,
got to pay the rent, need to get my teeth fixed
and all the money's spent.

You can feed my chicken and you can milk my cow,
       I feel free, I feel free anyhow!

Dance in the alley,
tror on the moon,
hop-along like Cassidy
in streets at high noon!

Walk on the waters, jump on a cloud,
       I feel free and I'm singing it out loud!

The clay is all frozen,
the pots are all cracked,
the kiln has exploded,
I ought to feel licked.

You can steal my paintings or tie them to a swing,
       I feel free like a bird on the wing!

Pick up a posy,
chew on a weed,
drink up the star-dust,
make hay in the reed!

You can take my stories and nick my alphabet.
        I feel free, I feel free of the net!

The teachers are silly,
and Thatcher's a guy,
the pope has drunk poison
and Trump is a spy.

You can see me naked and you can see me clad,
        I feel free, yeah, and I ain't been had!

Sing a song of sixpence,
warble in a brook,
whistle on a mountain
for every eye to look.

You can keep my songs for every I to see.

I feel free,

  I feel free,

    I feel free!

SCAPEGOAT ROCK I

a rocky-bluesy
type of song

Oh, here we go again,
I hear them everywhere I go:
"Wow, have you heard the latest news
of darling Romeo?"
And, bla, bla, bla, they all accuse him
of all kinds of sins.
They all feel shocked, they all pretend
they've been seduced by him.
Don't dare to look or cast a glance
at their own heart's desires,
they all fake shame, they all find blame,
shoutin' "More coal to the fires!"

> How come you're always dishin' out the dirt?
> Don't you know what Mary did?
> She didn't breathe a word!

Your'e lookin' so dumbfounded again,
been gobblin' up the news:
"The banks are busted, the rich guy's accosted," –
you feel yourself accused.
All day you blabber about
the burnin' question of the hour.
If you don't get to see it again on tv,
your stomach juices turn sour.
This time I'll skip the merry-go-round,
I think I'll stay behind.
Brother, I don't care no more
for a kaleidoscope of this kind!

> How come you always act so stupefied?
> To save the boys the fairy-tale girl
> nor talked, nor laughed, nor cried!

The Ripper's roamin' the streets again,
the whore made off with the clown.
Schwarzenegger's a fag, Madonna's a hag,
Guns n' Roses the talk of the town.
You're gossipin' it in the courtroom,
you're rattlin' it in the Met!
Golly gee, can't you ever try
to remember to forget?
The rat's killed a snake in a dungeon's
the thought you're tryin' to engender.
Please get outa my way, there's something important
I'm tryin' to remember!

> You're screamin' now, your tongue's all twisted too!
> But on the cross He said: "Forgive!
> They know not what they do."

SCAPEGOAT ROCK II

Crunch, smash, bang, crash rock

You're bustin' my brain,
you're gettin' it cracked,
you've got me slain,
your words are well-stacked.
       Don't want a discussion,
       feels like a concussion
       always talkin' things over.
       Yeah, please leave it, lover!
       No more last words!

I'm placed in a space where no thoughts can be heard.

You always complain
I don't think of you,
and that I'm to blame
that your dreams don't come true.
       Don't want a confession,
       it ain't my profession,
       yeah, please hit the sack,
       no more yakity yak.
       You're probably right!

But there's nobody perfect that's not out of sight.

I'm sick of your treat –
always beatin' me with words.
For once try go beat
your own self up first!
       Don't want conversation,
       don't feel no elation
       in words that don't give.
       You're too talkative.
       Don't ship me this violence!

For nothing is pure except within silence.

Please drop your slang,
I ain't no admirer
of your words' Big Bang –
feels like a quagmire.
> Can't take no more of it,
> you're really a hypocrite
> if you think that it's right –
> me to bask in your slight.
> Your words don't ring true!

I'm workin' for life and a love that breaks through!

GONE FISHIN'

Romanza molto ondulato

Swim pretty fish deep into your stream.
Please bring back to me a silvery dream.
I'll hang it up high in the top of a tree,
    and it's you, and it's you, and it's you, and it's you that I see.

Swim angel-fish deep into your pond
and bring me a sparkling mirage to taunt
me with flowery fairy-land fantasies,
    and it's you, and it's you, and it's you, it is you that I see.

Pretty blue fish swim away to the ocean
and bring home a mother-of-pearly illusion,
and let its light lustrously mesmerize me,
    and it's you, and it's you, and it's you, and it's you that I see.

Swim little white fish away to the sea –
please bring back a shimmering vision to me.
I'll climb to the roof-top and let it wave free,
    and it's you, and it's you, and it's you, it is you that I see.

Please pretty gold-fish dive into your fountain
and bring me a Fata Morgana, too haunting
for sight, yet evoking a sweet rhapsody,
    and it's you, and it's you, and it's you, and it's you

Swim all you fishes, swim if you can
and bring home to me a wonderful man.
I hold my arms round him and he holds me too,
    and it's you, and it's you, and it's you, and it's you, and it's you,

and it's you
       and it's you
             and it's you
                  and it's you
                       and it's you .....

MY LOVE (A SIMPLE SONG OF LOVE)

andantino maestoso

My love is like a mountain
made of solid gold.
My love is like a mountain
made of solid gold.
Though he's often far away,
he never leaves me cold.

:/:   My love is like a flower
that blossoms when he's near, :/:
and when he goes the sweetest scent
still lingers in the air.

:/:   Two lamps of love his eyes are,
they shine the brightest blue, :/:
and when he's gone the sky above
reminds me of their hue.

:/:   His voice is sweet as honey,
as silky soft as cream. :/:
It soothes me – it surrounds me
and shrouds me in my dreams.

:/:   There's music in his movements,
a song in every step, :/:
and I swoon, I melt, I tremble
each time I kiss his lips.

:/:   Each time I see him coming
my heart flies out to him. :/:
He's crept into my lifeblood,
love fills me to the brim.

:/:   He stands there in the doorway –
my house lights up in smiles. :/:
He wraps his arms around me
and says he'll stay a while.

:/:   And when he's got to leave me,
and when he says adieu, :/:
I know he's thinking of me,
I know his love is true.

:/:   Each time I light a candle
he lights up in my mind. :/:
A melody inside of me
sings we're two of a kind.

My love is like the eagle
soaring high and free.
My love is like the eagle
soaring high and free.
And when he's done his roundabouts
he spins right back to me.

MARY'S LAMB

To be sung to the melody of "Mary had a little lamb", jazzed up in a rock-a-by-baby hard-rock version.

Mary had a little lamb, little lamb, little lamb,
Mary had a little lamb,
its fleece was black as coal.
And everywhere that Mary went, Mary went, Mary went,
and everywhere that Mary went,
she stubbed her pure white soul.

:/: Mary was a witty girl :/: witty girl :/: :/:
she had a lot of charm.
:/: The lamb was always by her side, :/: by her side, :/: :/:
protecting her from harm.

:/: Mary played around with boys, :/: around with boys, :/: :/:
– she had a tomboy's heart.
:/: But when they'd messed around with her, :/: around with her, :/: :/:
the lamb it gave a start.

:/: Well, Mary liked to get her kicks, :/: get her kicks, :/: :/:
but the black lamb always loved her.
:/: While she was showing off her tricks, :/: off her tricks :/: :/:
the lamb was thinking of her.

:/: Mary had a girlfriend though, :/: girlfriend though :/: :/:
who was the teacher's pet.
:/: but every time that she came by, :/: she came by :/: :/:
the little black lamb wept.

:/: Her girlfriend was a a jealous sort, :/: jealous sort, :/: :/:
makin' out to be her saviour,
:/: she told the teacher all she knew, :/: all she knew, :/: :/:
'bout Mary's 'bad' behaviour.

:/: But Mary's little lamb, you know, :/: lamb, you know, :/: :/:
was hiding right nearby,
:/: and heard the words that had been said ,:/: had been said, :/: :/:
and silently it cried.

:/: Mary's teacher, gray and mean, :/: gray and mean, :/: :/:
she was the devil's fool:
:/: "If you don't stop your dealings, dear, :/: dealings, dear, :/: :/:
we'll run you out of school.

:/: "You've set a bad example now, :/: example now, :/: :/:
you know we just can't keep
:/: such crazy kids as you around, :/: you around, :/: :/:
you are the school's black sheep.

:/: Well, Mary didn't care two hoots, :/: care two hoots, :/: :/:
she wandered off in spite.
:/: The lamb it followed close behind, :/: close behind, :/: :/:
—   they walked into the night.

:/: They thought that she'ld be in for it, :/: in for it, :/: :/:
 but she never came to harm! —
:/: she had her black lamb by her side, :/: by her side, :/: :/:
 it was her lucky charm!

HELLO, MR. MEDICINE MAN

molto cantabile

Hello, Mr. Medicine Man,
put on your medicine hat, for
we're trapped in a witche's cage,
pretty fat, still getting fatter.
Loki's in the sewer
with his sons, the Wolf and Dragon,
loading skulls and bones unto
a million dollar wagon.

What cures have you in store
for the ills of mankind?
I can't see you anymore –
you're too far behind.
I guess it's too late now
and I've got to go.
Got to get ready for the show.

Hello, Mr. Medicine Man,
put on your medicine hat, for
the king's in a dismal dungeon
beating up the knaves there.
The red queen's in the parlor
counting bloody money,
and the maid is in the bathtub
drowning in the honey.

What balm have you in mind
For the wiles of mankind?
You're so hard to find,
you're lagging behind.
But I've got to leave you,
you're pace is too slow.
Got to get ready for the show.

Hello, Mr. Medicine Man,
put on your medicine hat, for
the Wolf is in the courtyard
hounding the kiddies pets there.
The Dragon's in the garden
chasing all the boys,
and Loki's in the romper room
breaking all their toys.

      What draught have you got
      for the scares of this lot?
      You're not really shot,
      you're just hard to spot.
      But I've got to leave you,
      yeah, I'm rarin' to go.
      Got to get ready for the show.

Hello, Mr. Medicine Man,
put on your medicine hat, for
the babies have been up all night
swallowing down the horrors.
They're watching it on the tv, where
they see mom massacred.
They also get the tidbits of
how Dracula Daddy's cured.

      What cure do you know
      for the gore of mankind?
      Kids are watching these shows
      and nobody minds.
      Not even the blackheads
      or the president's men
      will ever piece them
      together again.
      Now, what drug have you got
      for this dopy lot
      when junkfood impressions
      induce every thought?

Well, I gotta dress up,
I'm fixin' to fly –
to see the big blow-up
next Fourth of July.

Hello, Mr. Medicine Man,
put on your medicine hat, for
the Masters of the Universe
are rigging up their Ram-men.
They revel in the Devil,
while God's clear outa sight,
with special-effectual nightmares
to juice it up tonight.

But what can you do Mr. Medicine Man?
These 'Healthfood' impressions
are all a big sham.
But we've got crack –
crackin' up from inside,
and the manslaughter's caught on –
all-American landslide.
And though Georgie Porgie
Pudding and Pie
and all of his buddies
never told a lie,
we'll all see America,
yeah, the whole world fly high –
we'll get it together
next Fourth of July!

(... and there'll be spies in the sky when we die, goodbye!)

A LULLABY FOR CAROLINE

(Per vesperem ad astra)

andantino

Sweet babe Caroline   = *Ca-ro-lee-nuh*
peep into your mirror
you're complete and immeasurably pure.
No one can contest you,
no one can possess you,
and none can outrace you, for sure.

You were born of a love
that was lighter than light,
you were born with the stars in your eyes,
to show you, to lead you,
to know how to feed you
and read you the secrets of time.

Rustle and shake,
silver and gold,
you know there's a wisdom you hide.
It's locked up within you
to clean up the tinsel
that will constantly be by your side.

Look round about you
and don't be afraid –
your illusions will fall to the floor.
Don't try to mend them,
don't try to defend them,
and don't go 'round looking for more.

Peep into your mirror,
all others beside you
seem to be dark and obscure,
but though murky waters
will force you to falter,
get up and don't lock up your door.

When you see crazy madness,
don't let it blind you –
leave it be, and let the pain pass.
It seems larger than life,
but don't let it knife you,
for it's really more fragile than glass.

Rustle and shake,
gold and silver,
you know that you have been blessed
with the power of giving
new life to the living,
and the measures to drive away death.

Shake and rustle,
silver and gold,
you know that you've been infused
with a wanting to speedily
aid all the needy,
and keep them from being abused.

Backwards peep,
when men's sighs surround you –
you know they'll be coming in droves.
Your beautiful foliage
and their carnal knowledge
must meet, it's instilled – nature's law.

Backwards peep,
there's no blood on your slipper –
remember to treasure the hour.
But don't let it obsess you,
don't let it digest you,
and make sure it be tainted with love.

Rustle and shake,
you'll be disappointed
if you're looking to find just the man
who'll always adore you,
and keep your life for you –
then go back to where you began.

You're one in a million,
a pearl, Caroline,
and I'll bet you a million to one
that although people hurt you,
deny or desert you,
you'll still make it all the way home.

Yes, silver and gold –
you're one in two million,
and I'll bet you four million to two,
that if people reject you,
despise or deject you,
the light you ignite sees you through.

Oh, starry-eyed child
of the inward vision,
let it never deflect from your soul.
Don't ever forget
and don't let the sun set
on the promised land that you hold.

ON THE VERGE

allegro scherzando

You say I'm a liar,
you call me a thief.
I ought to be suave –
that's your belief.
What's it to you
if I'm puttin' on airs?
And maybe it's true,
but you're not bein' fair
when you say that I stole all your words
          and your favorite books.

          I'm tryin' for Zero
          to see the One,
          and though I'm noe hero
          I'll try for the sun!

You tell me I'm poutin'.
I say: Is that so!
You hear me shoutin'
when I keep my voice low.
And what's it to you
if I like to play games?
Nobody's winnin'
so why am I to blame
for gamblin' away all your cards
          and your janglin' dice?

          But I'm bettin' on Zero
          to toss up a One.
          Yeah, 'n' gee I'm no hero,
          but I'll try for the sun!

What's it to you
if I sleep on the job?
And why do you care
if I act like a slob?
You call me an egotist,
I say: What d'ya know!
You say I'm a deficit,
but it ain't fair, though,
and, okay, I've been pawnin' all of your
        grandmother's jewels.

        Still I'm headin' for Zero
        to land on a One,
        and sure I'm no hero,
        but I'll try for the sun.

Don't wanna play ball
to your pitch anymore.
Your balls are all foul –
I'll just walk through that door!
What do you care
if I like to roam,
when the thoughts that you shoot
never strike home?
You keep harpin' upon what you think
        all the others are thinkin'.

        I aim to hit Zero
        to strike out for a One,
        and though I'm no hero,
        I'm gonna make a home run –
        yeah, I'll try for the sun!

THE TWILIGHT ZONE

We're in the twilight zone
bordering on the day,
and I hear a crooner drone
about people whose bones
have been strewn along the way.

We're in the twilight zone
bordering on the night,
and I hear a lover croon
beneath a blue moon
about a love he calls his right.

We're in the twilight hour.
We're miles away from day,
and the sly coyotes scour
and offal devour,
and all slinky cats are gray.

We're in the twilight hour
one step ahead of night,
and zombies intermingle
and ghosts tingle
to the tempo of their plight.

We're in the twilight moment
one pace ahead of death,
and the mourning sighs
of hoot-owls' cries
prance upon men's breath.

We're in the twilight moment
bordering on life,
and in a murky meadow
a dank and hoary shadow
sharpens a gleaming knife.

We're in a twilight haven
where acts are wanton, wild.
All thoughts are dim-lit, shaven,
the feelings craven,
and the senses are beguiled.

We're in a twilight horde.
No sound reminds the mind
of the primal, mindful word
of an overlord
that's long been left behind.

We're in the twilight zone,
everywhere is strife.
No heat is kindled here –
just all-pervasive fear
of a gleaner's gleaming knife.

A LOVERS REGRET

Oh, hollow Day
when you went away!
Now I'm left all alone.
Forever gone is your love, and I long
all day and all night long
for your body, your kisses,
your heart on my heart − this is
worse than a curse of Hell's fire,
come, nurse my desire!
Oh, fallow Day!

Oh, dreary Day,
hear me cry in dismay!
Our love's ocean infinite,
and your breath and mine was one, limitless,
floating free, not a limit
was could part my soul and you,
nothing told that we were two.
Don't part my heart from this ocean,
come, spark my devotion!
Oh, dreary Day.

Oh, mournful Day,
don't make me pay
all my life, our loves
were meant to rise flame in flame,
to heaven, and one moment and forever
were content to flow together
in the smoke of our love's ether,
incensed innocently, past pretenses,
come, tune in to my senses!
Oh, scornful Day.

Oh, painful Day,
how could you betray
our life's hope? And now
my why-cries-rise-sky-high —
bring you back on my track. Come back to me,
don't let my tears drown me,
dense, black like oil. Come crown me
with life's beauty, love's attire,
come babe, light my fire!
Oh, painful Day.

Forgetful Day.
Why didn't you stay?
we were wont to be together
in the stream of our love flowing on
between the shores
of here today and evermore
where our minds and heartbeats throb,
flooding out all fault. Don't rob
our souls of the goal of our love,
come, lay down above me!
Oh regretful Day.

ODE TO THE SNOW

How I wish the snow would come,
white and light like eiderdown,
like a virgin wedding-gown,
come to cover up the ground
that surrounds me all aound −
where unfinished deeds abound −
so the things that I have done
won't be shown up by the sun,
and the things I haven't done'
won't run me down.

Oh, I beg the snow to come
and cover up the frosty ground,
who all barren, black and brown,
hides behind a purple frown.
Still she's hoping to become
carpet-clad in snow home-spun
by the North Wind whom all shun,
but by whom her burden's known
and who knows just how it's blown
out. She's his clown.

When one morning snow has come −
and I hope that day comes soon −
I'll shape three balls of snow and pound
and punch them tightly. There'll be found
a snow-watchman to guard my ground,
and in his chest, all white and round
my black heart's planted. When spring comes
my snowman's melted. On the ground
a blood-red ruby there's become
my new heart's sun.

I pray that longed-for day to come
when million snowflakes float on down
and gently cover sullen ground.
I'll lay me down upon a mound
and make an angel, lily-gowned,
who'll fly up high, my spirit bound
to her crown. And when she's gone,
when the snow's all melted down,
my strengthened spirit: Make it home
from heaven's dome!

IT'S A JOB – I'M SOLD OUT

Had a job in a factory, they bought my attention,
then I had another, what they bought I won't mention.
I was employed in a workshop, they had use for my skills,
I was hired by bureaucrats, they stomped out my will.
Had a job as a teacher, it just made me nervous,
I catered for the old folks at death row's service.
I worked as a dancer, they wanted my motion,
I slaved as an actor, they drained my emotions.
     And now all I do is just sit here and sing.
     Don't let it worry you none, I'm just doing my thing.

I worked in a hotel, but I couldn't stay –
the boss was too greedy, so the job didn't pay.
Had a go at computers, but the job made me dizzy,
started tending the bars, but the juice was too fizzy.
I worked in a tart shop, but I had to go –
the baker was sour-faced and I needed more dough.
It don't please me none working for nickles and dimes,
'n' though we all know loitering's the worst of all crimes,
     still, I'm painting my portraits and singing my songs,
     so just don't you worry, I'm tagging along!

They say bread should be bought by the sweat of man's brow,
yet I'm eating my pastry any-old-how.
And although poor man's made out of muscle and blood,
the cakes that I chew sure ain't made out of mud.
'Cause I've founded a new trade to pay for my time,
I followed the advice of the nursery rhyme.
For I'm just like a spy coming in from the cold –
from a rainbow voyage with that bucket of gold.
     And now all I do is just sit here and chirp,
     and the menu's all sugar and honey and syrup!

33

THE WANDERER

Acid rain is pouring down,
the wanderer's on the loose.
His face a mask, a twisted frown,
his neck's caught in a noose.
He doesn't see, he doesn't hear, and as I pass him by
my body freezes all my fear,
i swallow down a cry.

     And I hide inside a chilly wind −
     it jangles every nerve −
     and the question that is left behind's
     what purpose do I serve?

Acid thoughts are crowding in,
the wanderer's on the prowl.
He doesn't speak, he doesn't sing
and no one's heard him howl.
He sleeps where he can find a bed,
and when his hunger hits him,
he's known to steal a loaf of bread
to eat it when it fits him.

     And i hide inside a chilly wind −
     it jangles every nerve.
     The question that sticks in my mind's
     what purpose do I serve?

There's no one here can tell his tale,
there's no one knows his mind.
No one moves in close enough
to see what they can find.
No one even knows his name
or cares to find it out,
no one wants to know his game
or what his life's about.

And I hide inside a chilly wind —
it jangles every nerve.
The question that's stuck in my mind's
what purpose do I serve?

Acid vapours cloud my sight,
the wanderer's up ahead.
All movement stops, I lose my props,
I feel a panic dread.
His face is blank, expressionless,
his thoughts can't be determined.
His feelings, always unexpressed —
a secret-service-sermon.

And I hide inside a chilly wind —
it jangles every nerve.
The question jangles up my mind:
What purpose do I serve?

ACACIA

Where will you look
to find the wisdom of the ages?
You have read every book,
you have ransacked all the pages,
you've interrogated crooks,
you have scrutinized the sages,
it seems your trying to hinge a hook
on how to leap the seven stages.

      Then like a fruit on a tree
      the question came to me;
      like a present from the fairies,
      like Amen from Mother Mary:

Have you come to the point on the bridge of no return?
Are you really out of joint and are you badly burned?
      – or will you sacrifice your innocent Mimosa
      to avoid a life of 'Via Dolorosa'?

If you're determined, you'll find out
– your sleep, alone, defies it –
whether holler, scream or shout,
or burgle, beg or buy it,
and though you're caught up in a maze
where the music's roaring, raucous,
there's a thread bared in the haze
from (A)riadne to your (B)acchus.

      Like a fruit on a tree
      the question came to me,
      like a present from the fairies,
      like Amen from Mother Mary:

Have you reached the lake where past memories lie frozen,
where the image of your face breaks through: "Are you among the chosen?"
      – or do you elect to forget the fragrant, frail Mimosa
      for fear of facing 'Via Dolorosa'?

Where do you think you'll find
the first rung of the ladder,
or are you steps behind from where
your doings do not matter?
If you don't join your nature's kind
you'll lose your grip on the rudder —
then your stearing's out of time,
you'll wind up choking on your fodder.

> Like a fruit on a tree
> these questions came to me,
> like a present from the fairies,
> like Amen from Mother Mary:

Have you come to the crossing in the path of no control
where it's possible to wake and watch your life within unfold?

Have you come to the shores of the sea that's known to split
what's true from what is false to let falshood drown in it?
> — or do you think you'll lose your cherished, gold Mimose
> if you choose the hidden way of 'Dolorosa'?

Are you your own adept?
Advise yourself, go find a teacher,
go learn the dancing step,
and step ahead of past and future!
Then offer up your everything
and All will Now be given
in a moment's living quivering
from a love-bow, arrow-driven!

> Like a fruit on a tree
> the question came to me,
> like a present from the fairies,
> like Amen from Mother Mary:

Have you come to the banks of the river that divides
yourself from your self to show you all that your Self hides?
> — then why sacrifice the pristine, pure Mimosa?
> Love, pave the perfect path of 'Dolorosa'!

JUDAS BLUES

It's raining in Sahara –
the sand has turned to mud.
The sun is drying up the poles –
like drought before the flood.
The middle watch is cold and stiff
like calm before the storm.
The dogs' days are kept at bay
and no one feels alarm.
There's a hundred thousand hungry men
feeling fit to kill –
and they're killing children in Brazil.

The sign of the yellow dragon's
set in a ring of fire.
Smoke is crowding all the streets –
it's filling up the sky.
Dandy John is shouting out
for order to prevail.
Iron Hans is threatening
to throw the dregs in jail.
And there's a hundred thousand hungry men
killing on the sly –
and you can hear a twitching falcon cry.

The heartless hunters lead the game,
they think they're so damn smart
keeping wealth and poverty
ten thousand miles apart.
And upon all the nine-to-fives
they've cast their drowsy spell
of nine-day's-wonders-camouflage –
a non-apparent hell.
But there's a hundred thousand hungry men
calling kill or cure –
and they're turning children to manure.

The suit-and-tie-men gloat and boast
to the newsreel's photo-dud:
'We ain't done nothing bad at all,
it's them that's in the mud.
All we ever done is good –
for better, not for worse.
We can't help that we've been blessed,
it's them that have been cursed.'
And there's a hundred thousand hungry men
out there on the kill –
and they're killing children in Brazil.

Ladies hide your tender babies,
hide your young ones now!
The holders of the CIA have
come to hide your cow.
Don't let the tingling samba sounds
put you all to sleep!
The bankers of the IMF have
come to fleece your sheep.
But there's a million torn-up women
feeling fit to be tied,
and no lonesome orphan's high and dry.

Little boy blue is blowing his horn –
it's time to call it quits.
The lion and the unicorn
are champing at the bit.
And like Joan of Arc I'll sparkle,
I'll be the first in line
when the forging wave of righteousness
breaks through this wall of time
where a hundred thousand hungry men are
feeling fit to kill –
and they're killing children in Brazil.

I BELONG TO YOU

I want to go Nowhere very fast — to Ever-Forever-land,
and I'll get there by crawling under the skin
on the back of my lover's hand.

When his fist is clenched I'll creep into his palm — I'll make myself very slim,
so that every time he opens his hand
I'll be there to smile at him.

Yes, I'll make myself so small and slight he'll hardly believe that I'm there;
but for the times he wants me around
he won't have to kiss the air.

For Nowhere is somewhere out of sight of envious, prying eyes,
and Ever-Forever is everywhere
I'm in tune with my lover's sighs.

MARIGOLDS IN OUR HEARTS

Another kind of love in another kind of life
lives within the confines of my mind,
and in a wiser, truer world where I could be your wife —
never would I be so hard to find.

There goodness will not scorn us,
riches will adorn us —
all our life we'd never be apart.
Heaven will respect us,
angels will protect us,
and marigolds will settle in our hearts.

> *Living life together*
> *will open up vistas*
> *of vivid reflections*
> *of Eden's projections*
> *where wrong does not exist.*

For another kind of love with a multicolored light,
not to be debunked by busy bigots,
nurtures my reason with intravenous delights,
where even gravel-grinders churn out agates.

So give me leave to love you —
I would so purely love you
that shimmering jewels will see you duly crowned;
vestal virgins will restore us,
and oracles adore us,
so that love and you and me be heavenbound.

— Darling seek me out till I am found!

ALL IN ALL

Night and day will never merge and neither will the poles —
so while you're gone all I seem to do is fret and fuss
wondering whether Jupiter leaves Venus in the cold,
and whether the Almighty cares what will become of us.
But even though we're made to be a million miles apart,
you live within the center of my heart.

When my luck's deserted me and I can't find my home,
when all the friends I ever had have turned their backs on me,
and even when each thing in sight seems covered up in loam
so all my thoughts are purely grime that I refuse to see;
or when my life seems twisted and acutely curved and curled,
love is still the essence of my world.

The world is huge, the worlds are vast and wait to be discovered.
The stars are bright, each leaf is green, the owl flies by night;
each represents a universe whose meaning is well-covered,
yet all display a fraction of God's visionary light.
But, friend, until the final end you're my only goal,
because you occupy the center of my soul.

SUB ROSA

I never felt so fragile and forlorn
as on that winter's day you let me go.
It chilled my heart to see my dreams lie torn
and scattered on the cold and silent snow.
For though our infant love was like an ocean,
it seemed you turned your back on our devotion.

I sensed you didn't really want to leave me −
that fatal forces drove you to your goal.
Unwittingly, I thought that you believed me
to be the guardian angel of your soul.
But when you'd gone all nights were coloured blue
and all my days were empty without you.

Just like a displaced person seeking refuge
from life where meaning seems a past regret,
I struggled to create a second deluge
of images to help me to forget −
the flower of love that had us both amazed
stood frozen in a grey and bleary haze.

If love's a bloom that's not allowed to blossom
but stays a bud until its book is closed,
the earth had better hide it in her bosom
to keep the weeds from showing up the rose.
And so I keep you locked inside my heart
until that day you say we'll never part.

THE BELL – IT TOLLS FOR YOU

"Now listen here, you're wrong to be
so immaturely unaware
of world political strategies
and economical affairs.
You ought to sharpen up, you see,
go read some proper literature,
go study some psychology
to help your measly mind mature!"
Now this is what I told my friend –
we're sitting in that old café –
I really could not comprehend
where he had hid his brains that day.
All wrapped up in my mute ideas,
I started studying his face –
I'd used to think him beautiful,
I saw my judgment was misplaced –
his eyes were listless, cold and gray,
expression bitter, drab and mean,
his every feature spelled decay,
I wanted to escape this scene.
And as we sat there face to face,
my thoughts revolving, mind going dull,
I was really thinking to replace
this sweetheart with some other shell.

Then all at once I heard the church-bells ringing
from a brownstone chapel right across the street,
and within me another bell was singing
as if responding to a godly treat.
And now my self-sufficient thoughts had vanished,
my body all aglow in quiet joy.
My mind was purged; anew with love replenished
I looked into the eyes of my dear boy.
His face shone bright as if it had been lighted
up from within the center of his soul.
To part a part from likeness thus united
would be to trade the partial for the whole.

And for a spell time seemed as if suspended —
maybe the time it takes to count to ten —
but in that moment dual We had ended,
and only I am you, you I, was then.

Then silently time crowded out this seeing —
such unique vision cannot last for long —
I was reduced to ordinary being,
and I was placed in a state where I belong.
And yet I cannot drive away these questions,
they often wake me when I try to sleep,
they sometimes give me mental indegestion,
they speak: "Try these instead of counting sheep!" :

> Why must I always fight?
> Why must I always prove
> that I am in the right?
> And ever on the move,
> why must I always push —
> what do I stand to gain?
> Why must I shout and fuss
> forever and complain?
> Or have I just been curse?
> Why must I be above
> all others and be first
> when being last reads love?
> Is this some kind of treason —
> why isn't it on the shelf? —
> that captivates my reason
> and splits me from myself?
> What is this putrid leaven —
> can anybody tell? —
> that stays my way to heaven
> and enslaves me in this cell?

But wait, be still and listen now, I think I hear a bell :

Ah yes, but very distant, very fragile, faint and weak,
yet still quite clear
        I clearly hear
                a knell.

I REMEMBER YOU (A HYMN TO HIM)

LAST NIGHT I HAD A DREAM AND THERE I MET A TENDER YOUTH.
His face was shining, radiant, a harbinger of truth.
his skin was pure, his eyes were sure, with no trace of regret.
And golden ringlets framed his face, the fairest face I've met.
All clothed in white, complete.
>> I wonder what had made him come
>> to worship at my feet?

His face was shining, radiant, just lijke the sun at dawn,
and beauty was reflected from each thing it dawned upon.
His eyes' bright light shone steadily, his gaze was fixed on me,
and love, till then imprisoned, floated readily and free.
And the good youth stood my ground.
>> I wonder why it was he'd come
>> to heal my open wound?

His skin was pure, and in my soul it left a pearly trace.
No harrowed line marred his brow, now furrows maimed his face.
All lily-white and iridescent, glowing like the moon,
the knowledge poured from every pore: he hadn't come too soon.
But the youth had come before.
>> I wonder what had made him come
>> a-knocking at my door?

And golden ringlets framed his face, all gleaming like a crown,
all brilliantly sight-blinding and revealing his renown.
I stood there so constricted, my soul fighting to be free,
and he gave to me a secret key no one could give to me
except my loving Dove.
>> I wonder why it was he'd come
>> to honor me with love.

I STOOD SQUARE IN A MARKETPLACE, THE HOUR WAS MID-DAY.
And people swarming everywhere were all coming my way.
Their stares sliced me like daggers, each glare cut like a knife.
I stood stiff-frozen though I felt like running for my life.
And the good youth stood my ground.
>I wonder why it was he'd come
>to heal my open wound?

And people swarming everywhere, suspicion lit their faces.
Eyes were darting here and there, all jagged were their paces.
Though they were covered up in clothes all garishly refined,
it didn't help to cover their Medusa-gargoyled minds.
But the youth had come before.
>I wonder what had made him come
>a-knocking at my door?

Their stares sliced me like daggers, pupils all dilating.
Their mongrel thoughts pierced my skin, thoughts' arrows poison-plated.
Though they were wearing goggles, glasses, monocles and blinkers,
no one could protect my nose from smelling out these stinkers
except my loving Dove.
>I wonder why it was he'd come
>to honor me with love.

I stood stiff-frozen, realizing I couldn't even move.
Nothing in these half-breeds showed that my heart could approve.
My Ganymedes, my sentinel said: "They won't see you're here.
Just let me let you have my cloak – wear this and disappear!"
And still I wonder why!
>But his smile showed up *he lives in me,*
>as he said his goodbye.

AN OCTAVE OF LIFE I (A CONTEMPLLATION)

DO   BIRTH of my soul that ever You defend
is forsaken in me when the careless time I spend
attached to what attracts me – while my self has been divorced
from communion with You – runs down a *lifelike* course.

TI   LIFE in my world is spent in wild pursuit
of the happiness and riches I gain when I recruit
<u>envious</u>, partial thoughts in simple-minded purpose
of applying my *judgment* to achieve material surplus.

LA   JUDGMENT of myself I easily ignore
by hurling <u>angry</u> words against whoever's closed a door
and by avoiding disapproval when I pay the shameful token
of *silent*, fake agreement with the word that's last been spoken.

SO   SILENCE of my mind seems like a <u>slothful</u> burden
of formless shape and mass wherein my heart is hardened
in refusal to be pliable, like the clay you shape and fry,
to the command of the Creator for the *ego* to comply.

FA   DEATH of my soul's certain when <u>lusty</u> appetites
guide my senseless senses to hunt up sex-delights
in every hungry being, causing images to thrive
in fantasies of *love* that seem real and all alive.

MI   LOVE in my world shines whenever I fulfil
my <u>gluttenous</u> need to use others for my thrills
and when the mirror that I hold is constructed to reflect
the beauty of my body and to hide *<u>proud</u>* mind's defects.

RE   PRIDE of myself will ride me for a fall
when blind to Your light's guidance I won't bend to Nature's call,
but <u>avariciously</u> build myself a temporal throne;
then my soul's defeated and will meet a *birth* of stone.

DO   BIRTH of my soul that ever You defend
is forsaken in me when the careless time I spend
attached to what attracts me – while my self has been divorced
from communion with You – has run its lifelike course.

AN OCTAVE OF LIFE I (A CONTEMPLLATION)

DO   BIRTH of my soul that ever You defend
is fostered in me through the moments that You spend
in union with my self when my selfishness – divorced
from vainglorious greed – has run its *deadly* course.

RE   DEATH of my life creeps stealthily along
the path that is easily followed by the throng
of ambitious, alluring calls upon my love
that hide from my eyes *Love's* calling from above.

MI   LOVE of my soul is forever shed on me
by the power of Your mercy which often I don't see
when the thoughts in my mind build up associations
that feed my spirit rich with *proud* self-adulation.

FA   PRIDE of my self lives by the suffering of my ego
when gagged by Your presence it is humbled to let go
its vain suffering of opponents who constantly attack it
through its own proud contempt of all *life* that attracts it.

SO   LIFE of my death is always a dependent
on the light of Your love which leaves that life redundant
which eagerly I spend in chase of love and glory
restricting my soul to pointless, *judging* worry.

LA   JUDGMENT of my life is Yours, and Yours alone
is the self's silent invitation to atone
so that Your honor and glory will prove my life of violence
must suffer to surrender to gain the Throne of *Silence*.

TI   SILENCE of my mind that I may sense Your word
is all my heart may hope for when my vision isn't blurred
by sleepy dreams of me; then let my heart rejoin
that life, born of love, *rebirthed* in blood and wine.

DO   BIRTH of my soul that ever You defend
is fostered in me through the moments that You spend
in union with my self when my selfishness – divorced
from vainglorious greed – has run its deadly course.

LOT'S WIFE'S LOT

Once I turned into a pillar of salt
ignoring the Law when He said:
"Don't look back, it's not your fault.
Let the dead bury the dead!"

I raised my fist: "My fury's enlisted
and I want no other tutor
than the guarantee of the humility
of all our persecutors."

Then I heard the Lord's last words:
"Their destruction's already a fact.
I'll make you into a pillar of salt,
to forever witness the act,

if you try to see iniquity's fee;
your body'll be salified, frozen,
and the wisdom you gain will thus remain
as a salt-lick for the chosen."

"Just one last peek is all I seek
of our enemies' pain," I replied,
"I do spurn them and I'll soon return
to be by my husband's side."

Nothing stirred and not one word
resounded to my pleas,
but my recollection remained a reflection
of our flaming enemies.

And I couldn't believe that the Lord would bereave me
of my life in exchange for one glance.
I felt persuaded, if I didn't obey,
that He'd still give me one more chance.

So around I turned in anger burned,
I stood to witness the sins
of sexual abuse and avarice
be uprooted from within.

In shock I stared and everywhere
the lusty flames took fire.
They climbed the walls of houses and halls
till they could reach no higher.

I watched in fright into the night −
it was brighter than any day.
The howls and shrieks of the incensed freaks
would never pass away.

The noise that churned from flesh being burned
sounded their retribution,
as the gluttenous delights of the Sodomites
rent in complete execution.

And the screams and cries and inhuman sighs
roared in a deafening choir,
and mixed with the tunes of hell's bassoons
till the sound itself lit fire.

It startled my hearing, and my god-fearing
promise, now weak as wax,
was all forgotten for the sake of the rotten.
I was stranded in my tracks.

Little by little my nerves grew brittle,
my skin, it burned and itched,
and every cell in my body wailed —
I knew I was bewitched.

My muscles and fibres melted, expired,
with bone and marrow mixed,
and the energies that flowed in me
were thoroughly transfixed.

And little by little first one crystal
of salt, then another, shone clear.
Completely coherent and almost transparent
as a pillar of salt I appeared.

And here I stand forever banned,
as a symbol of deadly lust,
to out-wait doom — I've forsaken the groom —
I am the bride of waste.

I stand a reminder to all the blind
of the doom which will engulf us all,
if we refuse to listen to the voices that hiss
within our own bodies' walls.

I echo the words: "You're the salt of the earth,
but if it has lost its savour,
there'll be no rebirth, you're nothing worth,
turn back and taste its flavour!"

If you want to renew it, to taste it and chew it,
you'll find that it's always here,
it's on the ground, in deserts and towns,
it lingers in the air.

But in case you forget, I'll be standing here yet
to remind you to keep in touch
with the salt of your pride so it won't override you.
Then my name won't matter much.

In the heat of the night I'll be shining bright
for the seeker who wishes to see.
In the light of the day my form fades away –
you won't need me then, you'll be free.

ASTROLOGY APOLOGIA

My planets are in Taurus
but the moon's in Gemini.
The rising star's in Cancer
so moons keep floating by.
      Now you know why the butterfly's
      my secret favorite bird –
      she plays upon my heartstrings
      where her silent songs are heard.
            She always lands so peacefully,
            she's always right on time,
            and the fluttering of my heartbeat
            is an echo to her rhyme.

My fated goal's the waters
where life's a fishy dream.
The house I own's a friendly shack,
star-struck by flashing schemes.
      That's why the bachelor's button is
      my secret favorite knight –
      he heals imperfect vision
      when the blues are blazing bright.
            He teaches me to mingle
            and still remain as one;
            He's stamped my soul as single
            to reflect the steady sun.

I was born in the year of the Oxen,
and the earth is his employer.
The hour was the Dragon's
who needs eternal fires.
      Now you know why the elephant's
      my secret favorite cat.
      He always acts so dignified,
      he's ever where it's at.
            He always moves so easily,
            he never leaves a trace,
            and the trumpet blow of his warning call
            resounds in outer space.

Made in the USA
Las Vegas, NV
14 August 2021